MW00618866

GLIMPSE

NEW ORLEANS

Copyright © 2021 by Glimpse Guides.

Photographs copyright © 2021 by Jordan Rhodes.
Pages 178 and 180 constitute a continuation of the copyright page.

All rights reserved. No part of this book may be reproduced
in any form without permission from the publisher.

ISBN: 978-1-951412-12-8

Manufactured in China.

Design by Laurie Nicoud and Analia Pribyl,
The Creative Clique.

10 9 8 7 6 5 4 3 2

THE
collective.
BOOK STUDIO

Oakland, California
www.thecollectivebook.studio

luxury city guides

www.glimpseguides.com

@glimpseguides

Contents

01.

INTRODUCTION

NEW ORLEANS

We can't think of a more entertaining city than New Orleans, and although it has a nefarious reputation at times, it is actually one of the most kid-friendly travel destinations we have visited. Every iconic restaurant welcomes children, and the city offers endless amusements, such as trolley rides, an aquarium and a zoo, and jazz musicians performing in the streets. The whole family will love this beautiful, historic town.

Jordan Rhodes launched Glimpse because she found a gap in the luxury family travel space, and while these guides work for solo travelers and couples, we have written them for families, as well. Jordan loves introducing the world to her little ones, and we hope these guides will make travel with your own a bit easier.

Be sure to check out our website glimpseguides.com for current events and updates in each city (especially as some recommendations may have closed). You can also follow us on Instagram @glimpseguides.

New Orleans Guide by Jordan Rhodes
Design by Laurie Nicoud and Analia Pribyl

Please download the corresponding Glimpse app in the app store for maps of New Orleans with our recommendations highlighted, directions, current weather, the ability to save your favorites, notes, and quick access to contact information to look up hours of operation.

If you would like help planning your trip, please reach out to Glimpse Founder Jordan Rhodes at Jordanr@brownelltravel.com. Jordan is an ambassador with Brownell Travel, one of the most prestigious Virtuoso-affiliated travel agencies in the world, and would love to help further curate your vacation.

GIVE A GLIMPSE

100% of this guide's profits goes to our charity Give A Glimpse, which gives underserved students the educational gift of travel, whether sponsorships for study abroad programs, travel funding for internships, or travel funding for volunteer opportunities.

At Glimpse, we believe that travel is one of the most important forms of education. It has the ability to enhance young minds through connection, independence, and responsibility. More importantly, travel can help develop cultural sensitivity, compassion, and a sense of wonder. We believe that all deserve those experiences.

By purchasing this guide or any products we sell on our website, or by hiring us to plan your vacations through our partnership with Brownell Travel agency, you too are helping Give A Glimpse.

CLEA
Give A Glimpse recipient in Rome, 2019

ACKNOWLEDGMENTS

A huge thank you to Waris Ahluwalia, Lily Aldridge, Taylor Angino, Nicole Castiblanco Silva, Cece Villere Colhoun, Brenden Clark, Jasmine Contomichalos, Sara Ruffin Costello, Becca W. Flanagan, Claiborne Swanson Frank, Phebe Huth, Lauren Bush Lauren, Ian Malone, Laurie Nicoud, Barrett Norton, Roopal Patel, Laura Paterson, Analia Pribyl, Alexa Pulitzer, Julie Terrell Radford, Noah Rhodes, Glenn Shaw, Catherine Smith, Melinda Stevens, Catherine Tompkins, Claire Weil, Olivia Weiss, Khaki Wennstrom, Gucci Westman, and Anna Wintour.

02.

GUIDE TO
THE GUIDE

Each recommendation lists the address, phone number, and website (if available) and gives a simple overview. For those traveling with children, we have listed whether a restaurant has high chairs and kids' menus. There are also a few words listed to sum up each restaurant, including the type of food served.

THE GUIDE TO THOSE WORDS:

CASUAL
Jeans and flats are appropriate here.

STYLISH
Your outfit should be smart and sophisticated.

POSH
Men grab your coat and tie;
ladies, your heels.

CLASSIC
The décor is conservative and elegant.

CONTEMPORARY
The décor is simple and modern.

CONTEMPORARY/CLASSIC
The décor contains elements of each.

RUSTIC
The décor is most likely a bar setting.

CONSTANT
The spot never goes out of style.

HOT
This is the place to be at the moment.

03.

RESTAURANTS

JACK ROSE

BY NEIGHBORHOOD

*Can be found
in the Date Night
section*

ANTOINE'S

Address: 713 Saint Louis Street,
French Quarter, 70130
Phone: 504-581-4422
Website: antoines.com
Great for: BRUNCH, LUNCH, DINNER

Since 1840, Antoine's has been serving
exquisite French-Creole cuisine to New
Orleans elite in a beautiful setting of white
tiled floors and 14 private dining rooms.
Steeped in history, the oldest restaurant
in town is continuously one of the most
popular dining choices, and kids will feel
right at home in the rowdy atmosphere.

FRENCH CREOLE | CLASSIC | CONSTANT
UPSCALE | HIGH CHAIRS | CHILDREN'S ENTREES

ARNAUD'S

Address: 813 Bienville Avenue,
French Quarter, 70112
Phone: 504-523-5433
Website: arnaudsrestaurant.com
Great for: BRUNCH ON SUNDAYS, DINNER

Arnaud's is one of those visually stunning,
historic restaurants that feels like a step back
in time from the moment you walk in. Stained
glass windows, tiled floors, and intimate
tables make up the entertaining scene, and
like Antoine's, the noise will drown out the
sound of your children.

FRENCH CREOLE | CLASSIC | CONSTANT
UPSCALE | HIGH CHAIRS | CHILDREN'S ENTREES

CAFÉ DU MONDE

Address:
800 Decatur Street,
French Quarter, 70116
Phone:
504-525-4544
Website:
cafedumonde.com
Great for:
BREAKFAST, LUNCH, DINNER

RENCH MARKET

du Monde

EE STAND

Only the most truly devoted fans wait in the insanely long lines at Café du Monde, but having said that, many get FOMO if they do not get to try the famous beignets. Head over the second your kids wake up, and you may get in immediately. This is the original 1862 location and gift shop, but their website also sells beignet mix that can be shipped if you really don't want to wait in line.

CAFE | CLASSIC | CONSTANT | CASUAL

CAMELLIA GRILL

Address: 626 South Carrollton Avenue,
Carrolton, 70118
Phone: 504-309-2679
Website: camelliagrillnola.com
Great for: BREAKFAST, LUNCH, DINNER

It seems as though all New Orleans recommendations include many landmark restaurants, and Camellia Grill should not be kept off that list. This well-known diner has been serving locals since 1946, with a brief closing following Hurricane Katrina. After reopening under new ownership, it remains just as popular, and now has a second location in the French Quarter. Don't miss the cheeseburgers and pecan pie.

AMERICAN | CLASSIC | CONSTANT
CASUAL | ONE HIGH CHAIR–CALL AHEAD
CHILDREN'S MENU

CASAMENTOS

Address: 4330 Magazine Street,
Garden District, 70115
Phone: 504-895-9761
Website: casamentosrestaurant.com
Great for: LUNCH, DINNER

Famous for its authentic seafood, Casamentos is one of those super-casual spots that attracts everyone, from locals to well-known chefs, and has been featured on many TV shows. Open since 1919, this cash-only restaurant should not be missed if you're looking for a true New Orleans experience. Don't forget to order the raw oysters, and keep in mind they do not take reservations.

SEAFOOD | CLASSIC | CONSTANT
CASUAL | CHILDREN'S MENU

"

NEW ORLEANS

FOOD IS AS

DELICIOUS AS THE

LESS CRIMINAL FORMS

OF SIN.

Mark Twain

CLANCY'S

Address:
6100 Annunciation Street,
Audubon, 70118
Phone:
504-895-1111
Website:
clancysneworleans.com
Great for:
LUNCH, DINNER

Constantly recommended by locals as their
favorite place to get a meal, Clancy's has
been packed since its opening in the 1940s.
While fine for kids, and they do have one
high chair, the restaurant and bar can get
a bit cramped (in a good way), and adults
may feel more comfortable calling a sitter
for this one. Be on the lookout for famous
residents, including regular Archie Manning.

CREOLE | CLASSIC | CONSTANT | STYLISH
ONE HIGH CHAIR–CALL AHEAD

First Course

8 75
8 75
17 75
16 75
15 75

22 75

14 75
16 75
1

 Eggplant with Aioli Sauce
led Eggs Remoulade
 Remoulade
rs Bienville en Casserole
 Oysters with Brie
's Jumbo Lump Crabmeat Salad
ed Sea Scallops with Foie Gras and a
Port Wine Reduction
tta Gnocchi with Foie Gras and a
etbreads Facon du Chef
 and Ricotta Meatballs with Basil Pesto
 an Italian Sausage Bolognese
 and a Parmesan Broth
douille Sausage Gumbo

ade
ett Roast Be
inega

COMMANDER'S PALACE

Address: 1403 Washington Avenue,
Garden District, 70130
Phone: 504-899-8221
Website: commanderspalace.com
Great for: WEEKEND BRUNCH, DINNER

While some of our local friends can
sometimes find this spot overloaded with
tourists, the reason for the tourists is the
wow factor. Commander's Palace is a city
landmark. Founded in the late 1800s, it
has won seven James Beard Awards and
is the most popular spot for weekend jazz
brunches. Don't miss out on the famous
turtle soup or pecan pie.

CREOLE | CLASSIC | CONSTANT
UPSCALE | HIGH CHAIRS |V CHILDREN'S MENU

COMPERE LAPIN

Address: 533 Tchoupitoulas Street,
Warehouse District, 70130
Phone: 504-599-2119
Website: comperelapin.com
Great for: SUNDAY BRUNCH, DINNER

Chef Nina Compton is known for her
flavorful dishes, but also for her philosophy
that meals should create memories, and she
is consistently awarded for her talent. For
those reasons, Compere Lapin is the perfect
dining spot; *Esquire* hailed it one of the
"most important restaurants of the decade."
So what are you waiting for?

CARIBBEAN | RUSTIC | CONSTANT | CASUAL
HIGH CHAIRS | CHILDREN'S MENU

A GLIMPSE

One of America's first mixed cocktails
is the Sazerac, which was created by
Antoine Peychard in a bar in the
French Quarter.

GALATOIRE'S

Address:
209 Bourbon Street,
French Quarter, 70130
Phone:
504-525-2021
Website:
galatoires.com
Great for:
LUNCH, DINNER

Another New Orleans institution, Galatoire's is always a celebration, and this eatery is the recipient of a James Beard Foundation Award for Outstanding Restaurant. Don't be intimidated by the fine-dining dress code–in this city, fine dining means a party in a coat and tie, and families will love the exciting atmosphere. Like Antoine's and Arnaud's, the interior is a gorgeous mix of French and Southern influences, and the chef will work with you on dishes for the kids.

FRENCH CREOLE | CLASSIC | CONSTANT | UPSCALE
HIGH CHAIRS | VERBAL CHILDREN'S MENU

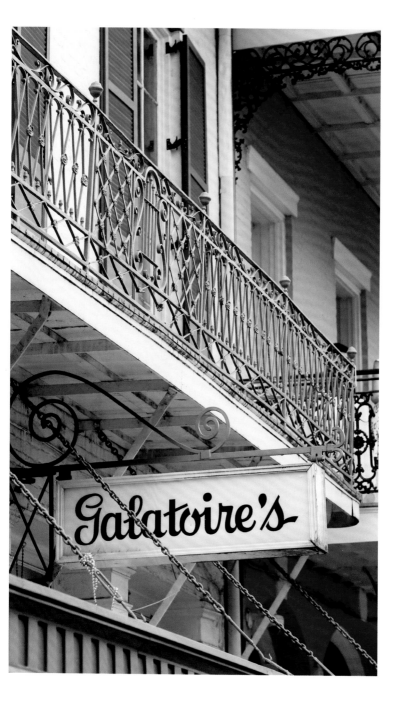

JACK ROSE

Address:
2031 St. Charles Avenue,
Garden District, 70130
Phone:
504-323-1500
Website:
jackroserestaurant.com
Great for:
SUNDAY BRUNCH, DINNER

We often talk about hotel restaurants in our Hotels section, but Jack Rose needs its own spot. This is one of the most visually stunning restaurants in the city, with bright colors, tiled floors, chandeliers, Ashley Longshore art, and velvet seating. We love toasting champagne in the garden and staying for hours on end—the website even encourages "spontaneous celebration." One of our memorable meals lasted five hours—kids not included for that one, of course.

ITALIAN/FRENCH/SPANISH I CONTEMPORARY/ CLASSIC
HOT I STYLISH I HIGH CHAIRS I CHILDREN'S MENU

LA PETITE GROCERY

Address: 4238 Magazine Street,
Uptown, 70115
Phone: 504-891-3377
Website: lapetitegrocery.com
Great for: BRUNCH, LUNCH, DINNER

A neighborhood gem, La Petite Grocery has
been the home of many different businesses
since the late 1800s, including—you guessed
it—a grocery store, until it turned into the current
restaurant in 2004. The outdoor seating on
Magazine Street is particularly popular, but
the indoor seating is where the scene is. In
2016, Chef Justin Devillier won a James Beard
Award for Best Southern Chef.

FRENCH | CLASSIC | CONSTANT | STYLISH
HIGH CHAIRS | CHILDREN'S MENU

LILETTE

Address: 3637 Magazine Street,
Garden District, 70115
Phone: 504-895-1636
Website: liletterestaurant.com
Great for: LUNCH, DINNER

Lilette is easily one of our favorite restaurants.
With the tiled floors, maroon banquettes
surrounded by mirrors, and gorgeous bar
commanding center stage, this French bistro
feels like a chic Parisian transplant. Plus,
we can never stop ordering the stone crab
claws with passion fruit butter.

FRENCH | CONTEMPORARY/CLASSIC | CONSTANT
STYLISH | ONE HIGH CHAIR—CALL AHEAD

LILETTE

A GLIMPSE

Oysters Rockefeller was invented
at Antoine's restaurant.

MAYPOP

Address: 611 O'Keefe Avenue,
Warehouse District, 70113
Phone: 504-518-6345
Website: maypoprestaurant.com
Great for: LUNCH, DINNER

You don't see many restaurants offering
Southern-Asian fusion, which is why we
recommend this creative alternative to the
other establishments in the city. Chef Michael
Gulotta is also known for another eatery,
Mopho, but this one is on the nicer side and
was named one of 2019's Top 10 Restaurants
by nola.com.

SOUTHERN-ASIAN | CONTEMPORARY
CONSTANT | STYLISH | HIGH CHAIRS
CHILDREN'S MENU

PÊCHE

Address: 800 Magazine Street,
Warehouse District, 70130
Phone: 504-522-1744
Website: pecherestaurant.com
Great for: LUNCH, DINNER

The description may sound cliché, but if
you're looking for mouth-watering, modern
seafood dishes, look no further than Pêche.
Local foodie friends swear it is the best
restaurant in town, and it's hard to disagree,
especially if you want a change from the
fine-dining classics in the French Quarter.
Bonus—the Louisiana Children's Museum
is just a block away.

SEAFOOD | CONTEMPORARY | HOT | CASUAL
HIGH CHAIRS | CHILDREN'S MENU

"

YOU'LL NEVER KNOW WHAT

HEAVEN MEANS UNTIL YOU'VE BEEN

DOWN TO NEW ORLEANS.

Elvis Presley

RESTAURANT R'EVOLUTION

Address:
777 Bienville Street,
French Quarter, 70130
Phone:
504-553-2277
Website:
revolutionnola.com
Great for:
DINNER

Restaurant R'evolution is consistently a spot
we return to over and over again with our
friends. The ambiance is vibrant, the interiors
are elegant, and it boasts a 10,000 bottle
wine cellar. But we cannot forget about the
food—Cajun and Creole at its best. While we
recommend enjoying this spot without young
kids, the Sunday Jazz Brunch would be the
best choice for the whole family.

FRENCH CREOLE I CLASSIC I CONSTANT
UPSCALE I HIGH CHAIRS I CHILDREN'S MENU

SHAYA

Address:
4213 Magazine Street,
Garden District, 70115
Phone:
504-891-4213
Website:
shayarestaurant.com
Great for:
LUNCH, DINNER

Another popular recommendation from locals is Shaya, a restaurant focusing on modern Israeli cuisine while incorporating Louisiana influences. Chef Alon Shaya works closely with local farmers to create his seasonal, responsibly sourced menus, while also relying on the traditions of his upbringing in Israel. If your kids are like mine, they'll love the hummus and pita bread.

ISRAELI | CONTEMPORARY | HOT | STYLISH
HIGH CHAIRS | CHILDREN'S MENU

ST. JAMES CHEESE COMPANY

Address: 5004 Prytania Street,
Uptown, 70115
Phone: 504-899-4737
Website: stjamescheese.com
Great for: LUNCH, DINNER PICK UP

Does one really need a detailed explanation to visit a cheese shop and café? St. James Cheese Company has you covered when it comes to all things cheese. Plus with sandwiches and salads in a chic space two blocks off St. Charles Avenue, it's the perfect spot to grab lunch on your way to Audubon Park.

GOURMET GROCERY STORE | CONTEMPORARY
CONSTANT | CASUAL | HIGH CHAIRS
CHILDREN'S MENU

THE COMPANY BURGER

Address: 4600 Freret Street,
Uptown, 70115
Phone: 504-267-0320
Website: thecompanyburger.com
Great for: LUNCH, DINNER

Opened by locals not long ago, The Company Burger soon became a huge hit among diners. Serving classic American cheeseburgers, milkshakes, and all the usual sides, it is a welcome respite from the city's typical seafood and French-creole dishes. Plus the counter service makes it nice and casual for the kids.

AMERICAN | CONTEMPORARY | CONSTANT
CASUAL | CHILDREN'S MENU

ST. JAMES
CHEESE COMPANY

A GLIMPSE

Popular New Orleans food includes
beignets, gumbo, po' boys, muffulettas,
and red beans and rice.

WILLIE MAE'S
SCOTCH HOUSE

Address:
2401 St. Ann Street,
Tremé, 70119
Phone:
504-822-9503
Great for:
LUNCH, AFTERNOON SNACK

This New Orleans institution has been popular since 1957, and in 2005 its legendary chef and namesake, Ms. Willie Mae Seaton, earned a coveted James Beard Award for "America's Classic Restaurant for the Southern Region." Come to this eatery located in the authentic Tremé neighborhood of New Orleans, for the best fried chicken you'll ever have and stay to converse with local fans.

SOUL FOOD | CLASSIC | CONSTANT | CASUAL
HIGH CHAIRS | CHILDREN'S MENU

"

NEW ORLEANS IS

LIKE A BIG MUSICAL GUMBO.

THE SOUND I HAVE IS FROM BEING

IN THE CITY MY WHOLE LIFE.

Trombone Shorty

04.

DATE NIGHT

BRENNAN'S

Address:
417 Royal Street,
French Quarter, 70130
Phone:
504-525-9711
Website:
brennansneworleans.com
Great for:
BREAKFAST, LUNCH, DINNER

Another New Orleans mainstay, Brennan's provides a more modern version of the classics. The multiple dining rooms showcase fine dining at its best, and the gilded chandeliers and ornate velvet chairs make you feel right at home in the deep South. This is also a great spot for drinks and dessert after a night out.

CREOLE | CONTEMPORARY/CLASSIC
CONSTANT | UPSCALE

GAUTREAU'S

Address:
1728 Soniat Street,
Uptown, 70115
Phone:
504-899-7397
Website:
gautreausrestaurant.com
Great for:
DINNER

Housed in a former pharmacy with no sign on the door, Gautreau's is a hidden residential gem and another choice for fine dining in New Orleans. Here the menu consists of inventive fish and meat dishes, and *Food & Wine* named three of the chefs "America's Best New Chefs."

NEW AMERICAN-FRENCH | CLASSIC
CONSTANT | UPSCALE

HERBSAINT

Address: 701 St. Charles Avenue,
Warehouse District, 70130
Phone: 504-524-4114
Website: herbsaint.com
Great for: LUNCH, DINNER

Herbsaint is a modern, upscale bistro located just outside the French Quarter on historic St. Charles Avenue. Serving an inventive fusion of French, Italian, and Southern dishes, diners will love the sleek interior and outdoor seating, and there is also a smaller bistro menu if you're settling in at the bar.

FRENCH-AMERICAN | CONTEMPORARY/CLASSIC
CONSTANT | STYLISH

MEAUXBAR

Address: 942 N. Rampart Street,
French Quarter, 70116
Phone: 504-569-9979
Website: meauxbar.com
Great for: AFTERNOON DRINKS, DINNER

This New Orleans bistro not only dishes out classic French cuisine accompanied by inventive cocktails, it also invites an eclectic mix of locals and visitors. Its location on the border of the neighborhoods of Treme and the French Quarter is part of what attracts this fascinating crowd, and we love the ambiance that comes with it.

FRENCH | CONTEMPORARY/CLASSIC
CONSTANT | STYLISH

"

THERE ARE

A LOT OF

PLACES I LIKE,

BUT I LIKE

NEW ORLEANS

BETTER.

Bob Dylan

SYLVAIN

Address:
625 Chartres Street,
French Quarter, 70130
Phone:
504-265-8123
Website:
sylvainnola.com
Great for:
LUNCH, DINNER

This gastropub housed in a carriage
house from the 1700s is where some of our
local friends like to unwind. Part restaurant,
part bar, the location in the French Quarter
is the perfect jumping-off point for a
night on the town.

SOUTHERN | CONTEMPORARY/CLASSIC
CONSTANT | STYLISH

THE COUNTRY CLUB

Address:
634 Louisa Street,
Marigny, 70117
Phone:
504-945-0742
Website:
thecountryclubneworleans.com
Great for:
LUNCH, DINNER

This adults-only restaurant (21+) is one of the most fun in New Orleans. Think drag queen brunches on Saturdays, cocktails next to an outdoor pool, and pre- and post-dinner drinks in an opulent setting. Be prepared to spend hours on end here.

ITALIAN/FRENCH/CREOLE/SOUTHERN
CLASSIC | HOT | STYLISH

05.

HOTELS

ACE NEW ORLEANS

Address:
600 Carondelet Street,
Warehouse District, 70130
Phone:
504-900-1180
Website:
acehotel.com/neworleans

A relative newcomer to New Orleans is the Ace Hotel, and for many it is a breath of fresh air among the more traditional, established hotels in the city. The 1920s building has been modernized but retains elements of that time period and attracts a clientele on the rowdy side. However, even though it become a nightlife hotspot, it's also good for families. There are busy restaurants, a music venue, and a rooftop bar, but next to that bar is a rooftop pool that kids will love. The rooms boast large windows and art deco influences, while the Ace Suite comes with a terrace, and some rooms come with guitars. For those who love to shop, there is an eclectic boutique downstairs, but the hotel is also just 15 minutes from the French Quarter.

AUDUBON COTTAGES

Address:
509 Dauphine Street,
French Quarter, 70112
Phone:
504-586-1516
Website:
auduboncottages.com

Often voted the number one hotel in
New Orleans, Audubon Cottages is an
oasis of seven beautifully decorated
bungalows surrounding private courtyards
and a heated, saltwater pool. Located right
in the middle of the French Quarter, the
boutique property is enclosed by walls, so
it is completely private, and guests will feel
like they're at an island hideaway, not a big
city. Each cottage is individually styled with
antiques—this is New Orleans, of course—
and comes with butler service. While fine
for families and convenient to many major
attractions and activities, call ahead to
make sure you are getting one of the
rooms that allows multiple kids.

A GLIMPSE

New Orleans has more canals, both above-
and below ground, than Venice, Italy.

HOTEL PETER AND PAUL

Address:
2317 Burgundy Street,
Marigny, 70117
Phone:
504-356-5200
Website:
hotelpeterandpaul.com

Hotel Peter and Paul is another newcomer
to the New Orleans scene, and one of
the most interesting concepts we have
seen. Housed in a former church built
in the 1800s, it also utilizes space in a
schoolhouse, rectory, and convent, all next
door to each other. We love the European
influences, like the detailed mahogany
staircases, claw-foot tubs, antiques, and
marble floors. Our personal loft featured
gingham furniture, a spiral staircase, and
luxe Italian sheets, but the vibrant Elysian
bar in the Rectory is where we spent most
of our time. The location is the farthest
hotel on our list from Magazine Street,
but it's a short stroll to the heart of the
French Quarter and in one of the
more underrated parts of town.

MAISON DE LA LUZ

Address:
546 Carondelet Street,
Warehouse District, 70130
Phone:
504-814-7720
Website:
maisondelaluz.com

Design lovers will swoon over the gorgeous interiors of the Maison de la Luz, with its sweeping double staircase, black-and-white marble floor, and antiques galore. The European features downstairs boast vibrant paint colors and dark corners, but the 67 suites are all individually decorated in soothing tones, and you will feel like you are in a home away from home. The living room, breakfast room, and bar are intimate yet exciting and the perfect places for a nightcap or pre-dinner conversation. If the weather suits, the rooftop bar is another great spot for socializing, or there is a salon reserved just for guests. While children are welcome, it might be best to enjoy this stay without the little ones.

PONTCHARTRAIN HOTEL

Address:
2031 St. Charles Avenue,
Garden District, 70130
Phone:
504-941-9000
Website:
thepontchartrainhotel.com

Another 1920s classic hotel is the
Pontchartrain, which is our less expensive
recommendation if you want to be right in
the Garden District. This historic jewel on
St. Charles Avenue is situated in the perfect
spot to venture around the city's grand,
historic homes, shop on Magazine Street, or
take a healthy stroll to the French Quarter.
It has been consistently voted the number
one hotel in New Orleans, not just for its
location but also for its public spaces. The
gallery-filled walls of the lounge area are
not to be missed—and include a piece by
famed local artist Ashley Longshore—and we
also adore the colorful restaurant and views
from the popular rooftop bar. After a night
of debauchery—or child care—the coffee
shop is a welcome site.

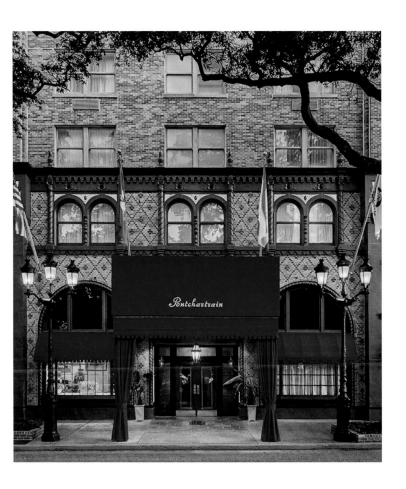

"

IF YOU LOVE NEW ORLEANS,

SHE'LL LOVE YOU BACK.

Drew Brees

SONIAT HOUSE

Address:
1133 Chartres Street,
French Quarter, 70116
Phone:
800-544-8808
Website:
soniathouse.com

Perhaps the most charming of all the hotels on this list, Soniat House is a true boutique hotel. Made up of several adjoining 19th century homes in the French Quarter, it features only 31 rooms, each individually decorated with period antiques. The hotel boasts a coveted location within the historic area, with a quaint central courtyard, balconies with intricate wrought iron railings typical of New Orleans, and a cozy sitting room with fireplace and honor bar. In case you happen to fall in love with the furnishings (you will), the owners opened an antiques shop right across the street. Breakfast is especially luxurious, as it is served on silver trays either in bed or in the courtyard, and the discerningly stocked wine cellar will meet the standards of all French and American wine enthusiasts. Children will especially love the house cat, Claire, but keep in mind that because of the small size and exclusivity of the property, only kids older than 10 are allowed.

THE CHLOE

Address:
4125 St. Charles Avenue,
Uptown, 70115
Phone:
504-541-5500
Website:
thechloenola.com

The newest addition to the New Orleans
hotel scene is The Chloe, designed by local
contributor to this guidebook, Sara Ruffin
Costello (see page 154). The Queen Anne-
style mansion dating back to 1891 features
just 14 rooms, as well as a restaurant known
as Parlor, which serves breakfast, lunch,
and dinner. There is also a chic bar, patio,
and swimming pool, but the best part of
the hotel is its location in Uptown. We have
always desired more glamorous boutique
hotels in this neighborhood, and we
finally have our wish.

A GLIMPSE

New Orleans was founded in 1718 by
Jean-Baptiste Le Moyne de Bienville. The city
was a fortified community on what is now the
French Quarter, and the streets were named
for French royals and the nobility.

THE RITZ CARLTON

Address:
921 Canal Street,
French Quarter, 70112
Phone:
504-524-1331
Website:
ritzcarlton.com

Ritz Carltons are always great choices for travelers, and the one in New Orleans is no exception. Located just on the outskirts of the French Quarter and right across from the launching point of the St. Charles Avenue streetcars, it is the perfect starting point from which to explore the city. One of the more kid-friendly hotels on the list, it features the coveted Ritz Kids club, designed to incorporate local elements and attractions into the activities they provide. The luxurious spa is a nice way to relax while the kids are enjoying the club, and a popular farm-to-table restaurant rounds out the glamour of the hotel, complete with a chic, spacious bar area and Parisian-style courtyard.

THE ROOSEVELT

Address:
130 Roosevelt Way,
French Quarter, 70112
Phone:
504-648-1200
Website:
therooseveltneworleans.com

One of the older hotels in New Orleans,
The Roosevelt is a luxurious Waldorf Astoria
property that was completely overhauled
following the damage wrought in 2005 by
Hurricane Katrina. The renovations brought
it back to its glory days when the current
property was first opened in 1907, and guests
will feel the history as they step through the
revolving doors and into the long marble
corridor with brass accents. The grand
restaurants and bars are known for their long
history of entertaining locals and well-known
guests, including such famous faces as Louis
Armstrong and Ray Charles. Children will
love the rooftop pool, and the holidays are
particularly exciting, with such activities as
a Teddy Bear Tea.

WINDSOR COURT

Address:
300 Gravier Street,
Central Business District, 70130
Phone:
504-523-6000
Website:
windsorcourthotel.com

Located a couple of blocks from the
aquarium, Louisiana Children's Museum,
and Audubon Butterfly Garden and
Insectarium, is Windsor Court, another
great hotel option near the French Quarter
that takes style cues from England.Perfect
for families, it is made up of mostly suites
with enormous bedroom and living areas,
complete with minibars and marble
bathrooms. Many also have balconies.
The massive, opulent lobby consists of
comfortable social areas, and an elegant
restaurant with English-themed adjoining
bar can be found on the second floor. The
hotel is also known for its world-class art
collection, and guests can enjoy audio tours
while children play in the rooftop pool.

"

NEW ORLEANS MAKES IT POSSIBLE TO GO TO

EUROPE WITHOUT EVER LEAVING THE UNITED STATES.

Franklin Delano Roosevelt

75

06.

SHOPPING
+ SPECIALTY
FOR KIDS

BANBURY CROSS
Address: 100 Atherton Street,
Metarie, 70005
Phone: 504-837-0447
Website: banburycrosskids.com

A bit out of the way, but the ultimate
Southern kids' clothing boutique with
smocked everything.

CREOLE CREAMERY
Address: 4924 Prytania Street,
Uptown, 70115
Phone: 504-894-8680
Website: creolecreamery.com

A cute ice cream parlor close to the
St. Charles Avenue trolley line.

BANBURY CROSS

FREEZY STREET
Address: 2633 St. Claude Avenue,
Marigny, 70117
Phone: 504-228-4149
Website: freezystreet.com

Kids love this hand-rolled ice cream
that is Thai-inspired.

HANSENS SNO-BLIZ

Address: 4801 Tchoupitoulas Street,
Uptown, 70115
Phone: 504-891-9788
Website: snobliz.com

A famous shaved ice and syrup shop,
open since 1939.

IDEA FACTORY

Address: 924 Royal Street,
French Quarter, 70116
Phone: 504-524-5195
Website: ideafactoryneworleans.com

Handcrafted, wooden toys and
games, among other items.

LITTLE TOY SHOPS

Address: 900 Decatur Street,
French Quarter, 70116
Phone: 504-522-6588
Website: littletoyshops.com

Love old-fashioned games and
hate plastic toys? This is the shop
for you.

"

IN NEW ORLEANS,

CULTURE DOESN'T COME

DOWN FROM ON HIGH,

IT BUBBLES UP FROM

THE STREETS.

Ellis Marsalis

MIGNON

Address: 5414 Magazine Street,
Garden District, 70115
Phone: 504-891-2374
Website: mignonnola.com

Stylish outfits and gifts for
babies and kids.

NOLA KIDS

Address: 333 Chartres Street,
French Quarter, 70130
Phone: 504-566-1340
Website: facebook.com/nolakids

This kids' store contains clothing, toys,
and a variety of other items.

PEONY

Address: 2240 Magazine Street,
Garden District, 70130
Phone: 504-300-7908
Website: peonynola.com

Gorgeous children's clothing,
plus chic gifts for all ages.

PIPPEN LANE

Address: 2930 Magazine Street,
Garden District, 70115
Phone: 504-269-0106
Website: pippenlane.com
An adorable, well-known children's designer
clothing boutique.

PIPPEN LANE

07.

SHOPPING + SPECIALTY FOR ADULTS

ADLERS

Address: 722 Canal Street,
Central Business District, 70130
Phone: 504-523-5292
Website: adlersjewelry.com

Where locals register for fine china
or purchase luxury watches, gifts,
and jewelry.

ANTOINE'S ANNEX

Address: 513 Royal Street,
French Quarter, 70130
Phone: 504-525-8045
Website: antoines.com

An outpost of Antoine's restaurant,
serving sweets, pastries, and coffee
in an old-fashioned shop.

AUX BELLE CHOSES

Address: 3912 Magazine Street,
Uptown, 70115
Phone: 504-891-1009
Website: abcneworleans.com

Handpicked home, garden, and gift items
from the English and French countryside.

BOUCANER

Website: boucanerwine.com

Look for this Southern wine, started by
New Orleans locals and co-founders of
charity event Hogs for the Cause, that
can be found in local restaurants such
as La Petite Grocery.

CENTURY GIRL VINTAGE

Address: 2023 Magazine Street,
Garden District, 70130
Phone: 504-875-3105
Website: centurygirlvintage.com

A popular vintage clothing and
consignment shop in town.

DRINK BEAUTY

Address: 3424 Magazine Street,
Uptown, 70115
Phone: 504-766-0873
Website: drinkbeautynola.com

Healthy coffees, teas, drinks, and
more in a cute setting, founded by
Glimpse contributor Cece Villere
Colhoun (see page 158.)

FAULKNER HOUSE BOOKS

Address: 624 Pirate's Alley,
French Quarter, 70116
Phone: 504-524-2940
Website: faulknerhousebooks.com

A beautiful bookshop in a building
where William Faulkner used to live.

FLEUR DE PARIS
Address: 523 Royal Street,
French Quarter, 70130
Phone: 504-525-1899
Website: fleurdeparis.net

Custom millinery in the French Quarter.

FRIEND & CO

Address: 7713 Maple Street,
Carrollton 70118
Phone: 504-866-5433
Website: friendandcompany.com

Custom and estate jewelry, china, and gifts.

GARDEN DISTRICT BOOK SHOP

Address: 2727 Prytania Street,
Garden District, 70130
Phone: 504-895-2266
Website: gardendistrictbookshop.com

There's nothing better than a quaint,
local bookstore.

JULIE NEILL DESIGNS

Address: 3908 Magazine Street,
Garden District, 70115
Phone: 504-899-4201
Website: julieneill.com

Gorgeous custom lighting fixtures.

LEONTINE LINENS

Address: 3806 Magazine Street,
Garden District, 70115
Phone: 504-899-7833
Website: leontinelinens.com

Iconic custom linens, plus beautiful gifts.

MAGAZINE STREET

This 6-mile stretch of antique shops
and boutiques is one reason to visit
New Orleans.

"

EVERY TIME I CLOSE

MY EYES BLOWING THAT

TRUMPET OF MINE, I LOOK

RIGHT INTO THE HEART OF

GOOD OLD NEW ORLEANS.

IT HAS GIVEN ME SOMETHING

TO LIVE FOR.

Louis Armstrong

MARTIN LAWRENCE GALLERY

Address: 433 Royal Street,
French Quarter, 70130
Phone: 504-299-9055
Website: martinlawrence.com

A high-end gallery with pieces by
artists such as Picasso and Warhol.

MASKARADE

Address: 630 St. Ann Street,
French Quarter, 70116
Phone: 504-568-1018
Website: themaskstore.com

Custom-designed masks for all occasions.

PILOT/POWELL

Address: 3901 Magazine Street,
Garden District, 70115
Phone: 504-827-1727
Website: pilotandpowell.com

A luxury boutique with designer
clothing, accessories, and shoes.

ROYAL STREET

One of the oldest streets in New Orleans,
full of antique stores and art galleries.

RUBENSTEIN BROTHERS

Address: 102 St. Charles Avenue,
Central Buisness District, 70130
Phone: 504-581-6666
Website: rubensteinsneworleans.com

Upscale menswear.

SHOP FREDA

Address: 600 Carondelet Street #130,
Warehouse District, 70130
Phone: 504-309-7515
Website: shop-freda.com

An eclectic selection of clothing, jewelry,
gifts, and more in the Ace Hotel.

SUNDAY SHOP

Address: 2025 Magazine Street,
Garden District, 70130
Phone: 504-342-2087
Website: sundayshop.co

Beautiful home decor, textiles, and gifts.

WILLA JEAN

Address: 611 O'Keefe Avenue,
Warehouse District, 70113
Phone: 504-509-7334
Website: willajean.com

An upscale bakery, café, and coffee
shop in a contemporary setting.

A GLIMPSE

New Orleans has the highest
number of historic districts in
the United States.

08.

EXPERIENCES FOR THE WHOLE FAMILY

AUDUBON AQUARIUM
OF THE AMERICAS

Address: 1 Canal Street,
French Quarter, 70130
Phone: 504-565-3033
Website: auduboninstitute.org

One of the top aquariums in the country
and a popular choice for families.

AUDUBON BUTTERFLY GARDEN
AND INSECTARIUM

Address: 423 Canal Street,
French Quarter, 70130
Phone: 504-524-2847
Website: auduboninstitute.org

North America's largest insect museum,
plus thousands of butterflies.

AUDUBON PARK AND ZOO

Address: 6500 Magazine Street,
Uptown, 70118
Phone: 504-861-2537
Website: auduboninstitute.org

Home to 2000 animals spread
across 58 acres.

CARRIAGE TOURS WITH
ROYAL CARRIAGES

Address: 700 Decatur Street,
French Quarter, 70116
Phone: 504-943-8820
Website: neworleanscarriages.com

Kids will love riding in a carriage
through the French Quarter.

CITY SIGHTSEEING
NEW ORLEANS

Phone: 504-207-6200
Website: citysightseeingneworleans.com

Hop-on hop-off double-decker
bus tours, with free walking tours
of the Garden District, French Quarter,
and Lafayette Cemetery #1.

GAMBIT

Website: bestofneworleans.com/current

Weekly magazine listing the city's upcoming
entertainment offerings. Copies can be found
at The Roosevelt Hotel and Antoine's Annex,
and other popular locations, or online.

HOGS FOR THE CAUSE

Website: hogsforthecause.com

One of the largest yearly BBQ and
music festivals in the country raises money
to provide monetary relief to families
with children battling brain cancer.
Occurs every March.

JAZZ AND HERITAGE FESTIVAL

Website: nojazzfest.com

Otherwise known as Jazz Fest, this music,
culinary, and cultural festival is one of the
most popular and well-known in the country.
Held every April/May.

LOUISIANA CHILDREN'S MUSEUM

Address: 15 Henry Thomas Drive,
City Park, 70124
Phone: 504-523-1357
Website: lcm.org

Playful and educational interactive games,
art studios, and a climbing wall in one of the
greatest children's museums we have seen.

"

I RETURNED TO NEW ORLEANS,

AND AS SOON AS I SMELLED THE

AIR, I KNEW I WAS HOME.

IT WAS RICH, ALMOST SWEET,

LIKE THE SCENT OF JASMINE

AND ROSES AROUND OUR OLD

COURTYARD. I WALKED THE

STREETS, SAVORING THAT

LONG-LOST PERFUME.

Anne Rice,

Interview with the Vampire

MARDI GRAS

Website: mardisgrasneworleans.com

The world's wildest party features parades, costumes, and debauchery. Hosted every February.

NATIONAL WORLD WAR II MUSEUM

Address: 945 Magazine Street, Warehouse District, 70130
Phone: 504-528-1944
Website: nationalww2museum.org

Children will enjoy this museum as much as adults, and there are often family workshops and overnights, so be sure to check the website calendar.

NATIONAL WORLD WAR II
MUSEUM

THE NATIONAL WWII MUSEUM

A GLIMPSE

The first Mardi Gras parade in New Orleans was held
in 1838. The parades are organized by groups known
as krewes who choose a different theme each year.

If you hear the phrase "laissez les bon temps rouler"
it means "let the good times roll" in Cajun French.
More than one million people visit New Orleans
to attend Mardi Gras each year.

NEW ORLEANS MUSEUM OF ART

Address: 1 Collins Diboll Circle,
City Park, 70124
Phone: 504-658-4100
Website: noma.org

Kids will find so many activities to do
here at NOMA, including baby workshops;
StoryQuest, which incorporates literature
and the arts; and many other studio projects.

RIVERS INSTITUTE FOR CONTEMPORARY ART & THOUGHT

Website: riversinstitute.org

The Rivers Institute is an online publishing
platform and kunsthalle, presenting
exhibitions and programming in New
Orleans and across the globe. Check out
the website for current events and exhibits
in New Orleans and worldwide.

STREETCAR RIDES

Website: norta.com

Three different lines take you all around
for $1.25 per ride. Check the website
for schedules and stops.

NEW ORLEANS
MUSEUM OF ART

09.

SAMPLE
ITINERARIES

These sample itineraries are appropriate for all ages. We have kept them light because we all know kids' moods can be unpredictable. For more age-specific activities, please go through our Experiences for the Whole Family section, which also gives more details on each recommendation listed here.

DAY ONE

MORNING

After breakfast at your hotel, which we find much easier to manage when traveling with kids who have woken up hungry (hotel breakfasts are also free if you book with Glimpse), head to the **Audubon Aquarium of the Americas**.

LUNCH

Nearby is **Pêche**, which features innovative seafood dishes.

AFTERNOON

Just two blocks away from the restaurant is the **Louisiana Children's Museum**.

DINNER

Galatoire's is the perfect end to your first day in New Orleans.

DAY TWO

MORNING

Start a science-filled day at the **Audubon Butterfly Garden** and **Insectarium**.

Afterwards hop on the **St. Charles Streetcar** located just across the street and head uptown.

LUNCH

Hop off at the Robert Street stop and grab a bite to eat at **St. James Cheese Company** two blocks away. You can also order food to go and enjoy a picnic at the **Audubon Park** after hopping back on the trolley.

AFTERNOON

Enjoy the park and the nearby **Audubon Zoo**.

DINNER

Head to **Commander's Palace** for a fun meal.

A GLIMPSE

New Orleans' St. Louis Cathedral is the oldest
operating cathedral in the United States.

If traveling without kids or just taking some time on your own (with the help of a nanny or hired sitter), we suggest the following itinerary.

DAY WITHOUT KIDS

MORNING

Spend your morning antiques shopping on **Magazine Street**. You also don't want to miss **Leontine Linens** for bedroom and bathroom updating.

LUNCH

Lilette is a great spot for lunch.

AFTERNOON

Explore the **French Quarter**, where more antique stores and art galleries await you.

The area has so many bars, you could walk into any of them for a cocktail and have a good time.

DINNER

Head back uptown to **Clancy's** for a fun dinner among locals.

LATER

If you're still up for some fun, head back to the **French Quarter** and enjoy the spectacle of midnight revelers and jazz musicians.

10.

CITY TIPS
+ HELPFUL
INFORMATION

While cars are not necessary here, you may want to rent one at the airport if you plan to explore the Gulf Coast.

If you do not rent a car, many of the hotels on this list are all in, or within walking distance of, the French Quarter. If you're heading uptown to places like the zoo, the St. Charles Streetcar will get you there, as will taxis or Ubers.

There are also carriage rides for exploring the French Quarter.

Magazine Street is a great 6-mile stretch for walking and shopping.

BABY FOOD, DIAPERS, ETC.

Pharmacies are great places for baby-related items. For organic baby food and baby items, head to Whole Foods on Magazine Street between Joseph and Arabella.

BABYSITTING

Each hotel we have listed is able to find reputable babysitters, but most of them require at least 24 hours notice.

BATHROOMS

There are public restrooms in the French Market near Café du Monde and the Audubon Park.

Many cafés are also great places to stop for a break since the bathrooms are often for patrons only.

EMBASSIES

There are a handful of embassies in New Orleans. To find a particular country's location, go to embassy.goabroad.com.

A GLIMPSE

New Orleans is the birthplace of jazz,
and a man named Buddy Bolden is said to
be the first to improvize with his trumpet.

HEALTH CARE

Children's Hospital of New Orleans
Address: 200 Henry Clay Avenue
Website: chnola.org

POLICE AND EMERGENCIES

In an emergency, dial 911 for police,
ambulances, and the fire department.

STROLLERS

New Orleans is a pretty easy place to get
around with strollers. Still, some restaurants
are tight, so call ahead to see if they can
be parked next to your tables.

"

DON'T YOU JUST LOVE

THOSE LONG RAINY AFTERNOONS

IN NEW ORLEANS WHEN AN HOUR

ISN'T JUST AN HOUR – BUT A LITTLE

PIECE OF ETERNITY DROPPED INTO

YOUR HANDS – AND WHO KNOWS

WHAT TO DO WITH IT?

Tennessee Williams,
A Street Car Named Desire

TIPPING

Tipping in America is customary, and 20% of the bill is normal in restaurants (although some places are beginning to include the tip in the total, so be sure to look for "gratuity included.")

Leave money for housekeeping in hotels.

For porters, about $2 per piece of luggage is normal.

For a concierge, leave money per reservation.

In taxis, round up to the nearest dollar and then add $1 or $2 for a tip. Obviously if you Uber, the tip is already included.

If you valet your car anywhere, give $3 to $5 when they bring it back around.

TOURISM WEBSITE

The official Office of Tourism website is neworleansonline.com.

11.

PACKING

When traveling, we recommend listing exact outfits for each day in order to avoid overpacking and to stay organized. We also encourage mixing and matching key pieces, so you have more room for purchases. We then place items either in packing cubes, or directly in the suitcase starting with the last day, so you are not digging for clothing packed for day one.

MAISON DE LA LUZ

DAY ONE

Morning: ....

....

....

....

....

Evening: ....

....

....

....

....

Kids: ....

....

....

....

....

DAY TWO

Morning: ....

....

....

....

....

....

Evening: ....

....

....

....

....

....

Kids: ....

....

....

....

....

....

DAY THREE

Morning: ....

....

....

....

....

....

Evening: ....

....

....

....

....

....

Kids: ....

....

....

....

....

....

DAY FOUR

Morning: ....

....

....

....

....

....

Evening: ....

....

....

....

....

Kids: ....

....

....

....

....

....

MAISON DE LA LUZ

NEW ORLEANS PACKING TIPS

Highlight or put a mark next to
outfits once they're packed.

Flat shoes are a must for walking
around the French Quarter.

DAY FIVE

Morning: ....
....
....
....
....
....

Evening: ....
....
....
....
....
....

Kids: ....
....
....
....
....
....

"

I GET IDEAS ABOUT

WHAT'S *ESSENTIAL* WHEN

PACKING MY SUITCASE.

Diane von Furstenberg

DAY SIX

Morning: ....

....

....

....

....

....

Evening: ....

....

....

....

....

....

Kids: ....

....

....

....

....

....

DAY SEVEN

Morning: ....

....

....

....

....

....

Evening: ....

....

....

....

....

....

Kids: ....

....

....

....

....

....

CARRY-ON

- [ ] Passport/ID

- [ ] Change of Clothes
  for yourself and the kids

- [ ] Bathing Suits
  *in case you need to change
  your plans on arrival, or in
  the case of lost luggage*

- [ ] Laptop/Tablet

- [ ] Jewelry

- [ ] Camera

- [ ] Converter

- [ ] Headphones

- [ ] Chargers

- [ ] Glasses

- [ ] Medication and Supplements

- [ ] Books/Magazines

- [ ] Snacks

- [ ] Travel Wrap

- [ ] Lotion

- [ ] Face Mist

- [ ] Lip Moisturizer

☐ Other: ....

....

....

....

....

KIDS

☐ Tablet/iPad

☐ Headphones

☐ Backpacks

☐ Coats/Jackets

☐ Snacks

☐ Toys

☐ Other: ....

....

....

....

BABIES

☐ Bottle and Formula/Milk

☐ Pacifier

☐ Snacks

☐ Blankets

☐ Toys

☐ Other: ....

....

....

EXTRAS

☐ Workout Clothes

☐ Coats/Jackets

☐ Lingerie

☐ Toiletries

☐ Other: ....

....

....

....

....

....

....

....

....

....

....

....

....

....

....

12.

TIPS FROM
THE EXPERTS

HOW TO GET THE MOST OUT OF
YOUR TRAVEL EXPERIENCES

BY MELINDA STEVENS,
EDITOR-IN-CHIEF OF CONDÉ NAST TRAVELLER

1. Plan, but don't overplan! The best stuff happens in the places in between–the surprises, the unexpected–being loose enough to go with the flow, so you can get happily caught up where the best experiences are unfolding, not with what the schedule dictates.

2. Travel, really, is mostly about the people. Meeting people in the place you have travelled to–having drinks with them, going to their houses, hearing about their lives–is what takes a standard trip and moves it onto a different level. Open your hearts and minds! Be alert to this possibility, even if you are normally a shy person. Find out where the locals dance, not the tourists, where they eat and hang out and shop. This will give you an infinitely better understanding of a place and a people who are different from you. Which is the point.

3. Take your time. Sure, it's fun to go somewhere for a quick jaunt. I went to Norway for 16 hours to see the White Lights, and I once seemingly went to Shanghai for a bath. But it's only by taking your time, stretching it out, being somewhere for any considered length at all that will unhook you from your normal schedule and allow you to be more expansive with your horizons, literally and metaphorically.

4. Reward good work. Choose to stay in places that have more than their own pockets in mind. How is your hotel connected to its community, how does it support it, is it known for its good works, in any variety of ways, from protecting biodiversity to adhering to sound sustainable practices?

5. Tread lightly. In all ways. You are a guest in other people's lands. Understand the rules, be aware and be curious, hold back on your brashness, pick up your rubbish, pay your way, be generous and thoughtful with your time and your money. Contribute and engage. Your tourists bucks are a powerful tool, use them in the right way. Be a good human making good decisions.

MELINDA'S NEW ORLEANS FAVORITES

Soniat House is charming as is the amazing
Hotel Peter and Paul, and Preservation Hall is the
real deal spot for New Orleans jazz.

BY WARIS AHLUWALIA,
ACTOR, DESIGNER, AND FOUNDER
OF HOUSE OF WARIS

1. Prepare. Mostly I think about food–traveling or not.
However, planes get delayed, road trips take longer,
etc. It's best to be prepared, so you're not forced to eat
junk food that's readily available everywhere in the
world. Pack snacks. Always. For me it's raw almonds,
raw cashews, low-sugar protein bars.

2. Hydrate. Bring a water bottle. Buy water. Whatever
the situation, drink water. Dehydration causes
headaches, makes you feel tired, and can lead to loss
of strength and stamina. You need strength and stamina
every day but especially when you're traveling.

3. Get Outside. Find the sunshine or at the very least
some fresh air. Go outside and feel the sun on your face.
It can help reset your body clock. Skip the nap and
adjust to your new time zone.

4. Exercise. Any movement helps me tremendously.
Healthy body, healthy mind. Use the hotel gym, go for
a run in the neighborhood, or find a local park. There's
nothing more grounding than the earth, grass, and trees.

5. Breathe. Deeply. Not the way we normally do,
with shallow breaths. But intentional, slow breathing.
Deep breathing can immediately lower your heart
rate and blood pressure.

WARIS'S NEW ORLEANS FAVORITE

Maison de la Luz.

BY ALEXA PULITZER, ARTIST AND FOUNDER OF ALEXAPULITZER.COM

FAVORITE...

Hotel:
Maison de la Luz
and Hotel Peter and Paul

Restaurant:
Paladar 511, N7, or Zasu

Clothing Boutique:
Peony

Home Decor Boutique:
Perch, and Dop Antiques

Bakery:
La Boulangerie

Specialty Shop:
Saint Claude Social Club

Spa:
Private masseuse–Mary
Jefferson or Horn Hom

Bar:
Bacchanal

Museum:
Historical New Orleans
Collection

Neighborhood:
French Quarter or
Garden District

Park:
Couturie Forest

Hidden Gem:
Preservation Hall

*If you had one last day
in New Orleans, what
would you do?*
Pick up café au lait and
beignets from Café du
Monde (in City Park) and
walk through the Besthoff
Sculpture Garden (also
in City Park), then walk
down Esplanade Avenue
to Frenchman Street and
listen to live music!

OPPOSITE
ALEXA, ON THE BALCONY OF THE
OLDEST APARTMENT BUILDING
IN AMERICA: THE PONTALBA,
OVERLOOKING JACKSON SQUARE,
WHERE SHE LIVED AS A CHILD. BEHIND
HER HANGS THE NEW ORLEANS
TRICENTENNIAL FLAG, WHICH BARES
THE LOGO THAT THE CITY ASKED HER
TO DESIGN TO COMMEMORATE IT'S
300TH BIRTHDAY.

SHOPPING TIPS WHILE TRAVELING

BY ROOPAL PATEL,
FASHION DIRECTOR OF
SAKS FIFTH AVENUE

1. Get lost! I like exploring local spots to find new shops when I visit somewhere for the first time. It's good to get lost and take your time. I have found so many treasures shopping this way.

2. Support and buy local. There is nothing better than discovering a new designer, artist, home goods ware, etc. for the first time. I always like coming home from my travels with a little keepsake that's special that reminds me of my trip.

3. Taste the town. I love to cook, especially new recipes I come across on my travels. I always visit the local grocery and bring back a few local spices, flavors, etc.

BY LAUREN BUSH LAUREN, FOUNDER OF *FEED*

1. Support businesses doing good.
Stay at hotels and resorts that prioritize more eco-friendly practices and community give-back programs.

2. Volunteer in the city. Find a local charity or community program and lend a helping hand. It could be a soup kitchen or a beach clean-up. It's also a good way to meet some of the locals.

3. Be active. Walking, biking, or taking public transport is a great way to get to know a new place, and it is also more environmentally friendly.

4. Explore art and culture. Support museums and other cultural institutions while traveling. Many depend on tourists' revenue to operate.

5. Shop local. Seek out the mom and pop boutiques and restaurants. These are also the most interesting and charming in my opinion.

LAUREN'S NEW ORLEANS FAVORITE

Soniat House.

BY SARA RUFFIN COSTELLO, INTERIOR DESIGNER

FAVORITE...

Hotel:
My new hotel, The Chloe.

Restaurant:
Lilette on Magazine Street.

Clothing Boutique:
Saint Claude Social—locally made clothes and jewelry and insane costuming.

Home Decor Boutique:
Sunday Shop—antiques and modern stuff. Great taste in a beautiful setting.

Bakery:
Beth Biundo Sweets—not only delicious baked items but little gifts from Morocco etc. Also can't beat La Boulangerie.

Specialty Shop:
Coutelier Nola—specialty knife shop. All the local superstar chefs shop here.

Spa:
Belladonna

Bar:
I like dive bars, so Vaughans Lounge in the Bywater or Parasol's or Petes Out in the Cold—both in the Irish Channel.

Museum:
NOMA—stunning example of tropical classicism with an interesting collection of blue chip, old world, and emerging.

Neighborhood:
The Garden District

Park:
Audubon Park

Hidden Gem:
Lower Garden neighborhood

If you had one last day in New Orleans, what would you do?
Sit at the oyster bar at Pascal's Manale and shoot the breeze with Thomas "Uptown T" Stewart— the best oyster shucker/storyteller in New Orleans.

BY GUCCI WESTMAN,
MAKEUP ARTIST AND FOUNDER OF
WESTMAN ATELIER

1. Travel light. Travel with an edited makeup bag—it should be clean, purposeful, and curated. Travel and fragrance atomizers actually inspired the packaging for my Westman Atelier products. I love how atomizers are small and portable but still beautiful and functional.

2. Hydrate often. I'm a big believer in hydrating the skin from the inside-out. For an extra pick me up, I'll add an electrolyte tablet from Nuun to my water. My carry-on is never without a hydrating bio-cellulose mask and a rich moisturizer.

3. Refresh yourself. If jet-lag is catching up to you, you can fake a wide-awake look. Start with a highlighter under your foundation for an ethereal finish. Apply foundation under your eyes, using a brush in an upward motion to lift up the corners of your eyes. Spot check any redness as well. Sweep bronzer horizontally over the areas of your face that naturally get sun—cheeks, temples, forehead and eyelids. Don't forget under your eyes too. Pop a little rosy flush onto your cheeks and lips, and finish with a coat of mascara on the lashes.

4. Reset your energy. If time allows, exercise and a quick lymphatic drainage massage do wonders for the body. If not, take a few moments in the morning to stretch and meditate—it will reset your energy and lift up your mood.

5. Be inspired. Beauty should always be fun! When deciding what to pack in your bag, be inspired by where you are going and what you are doing. Have fun and experiment!

BY CECE VILLERE COLHOUN, FOUNDER OF DRINK BEAUTY

FAVORITE...

Hotel:
The Windsor Court. In my opinion it's the finest hotel in the city. I mean, how can you beat the Polo Lounge?!

Restaurant:
I'd have to say Arnaud's. We had our rehearsal dinner there, and it's family owned for generations that we know and love. They are always so grateful to see you walk in, and the dining room is the most beautiful in the city. Something just feels right being so deeply rooted here, they never mess up a classic creole dish.

Clothing Boutique:
Pilot/Powell

Home Decor Boutique:
Sunday Shop

Bakery:
Probably La Boulangerie. The chocolate chip banana bread is sinful.

Specialty Shop:
Pied Nu. I love the John Derian plates I've collected from her along with my always resource for Diptyque candles.

Spa:
Glass Skin

Bar:
I don't drink, so bars aren't too much my scene, but I like Bar Marilou a lot.

Museum:
NOMA

Neighborhood:
The Garden District

Park:
Audubon

Hidden Gem:
The Tree of Life in Audubon park.

If you had one last day in New Orleans, what would you do?
Ride the streetcar from Walnut Street to the French Quarter, buy something unforgettably fabulous on Royal Street, and eat beignets. Oh! And have my fortune read, tarot and palm, by a gypsy in Jackson Square. But there never really will be a last day in New Orleans, will there? Marie Laveau made it that way, the creole voodoo priestess cast a spell on Nola water. If you take a sip, you'll always return.

HOW TO CAPTURE THE MOMENTS WHILE TRAVELING

BY CLAIBORNE SWANSON FRANK, PHOTOGRAPHER AND AUTHOR

1. Camera ready. Take photos on automatic setting or iPhone, so you don't miss moments.

2. Finishing touch. I love using an app called Camera Plus to crop, filter, and frame my photos. It's awesome and gives the photos a finished vibe.

3. Album goals. Set out to create an album at the start of the trip, so you stay focused and committed.

4. Snap, snap. You can never take too many photos.

5. Be present. Turn your phone off often and be present to the beauty around you. Take in the adventure and the precious moments you are living. You never get those back.

CLAIBORNE'S NEW ORLEANS FAVORITE

Soniat House, walking around the French Quarter, and eating beignets at Café du Monde.

TIPS FOR TRAVELING WITH KIDS

BY LILY ALDRIDGE, MOM, MODEL, AND ENTREPRENEUR

1. Snacks, snacks, and more snacks! I make sure to have their favorite snacks handy.

2. Call the hotel ahead of time. See what they provide in order to minimize packing (i.e., cribs, monitors, extra refrigerator for milk, kids snacks, etc.).

3. Never rely on your phone or airport wifi! Download movies, TV shows, and educational apps before arriving at the airport.

4. Middle section, please! On a redeye, I try to book seats in the middle of the cabin, away from noise and light.

5. Go with the flow.

13.

NOTES

NOTES

NOTES

NOTES

NOTES

___

NOTES

NOTES

" ONCE YOU HAVE TRAVELE

BUT IS PLAYED OUT OVER AND OV

THE MIND CAN NEVER BREA

HE VOYAGE NEVER ENDS,

GAIN IN THE QUIETEST CHAMBERS.

OFF FROM THE JOURNEY."

Pat Conroy

PHOTOGRAPHY CREDITS

Page 5 | Photograph Copyright © Clea Ramos

Page 17 | Photograph Copyright © Antoine's

Page 18 | Photograph Copyright © Phebe Huth

Page 25 | Photograph Copyright © Commander's Palace by NolaVid/Max Cusimano

Page 27 | Photograph Copyright © Galatoire's

Page 28 | Photograph Copyright © Jack Rose by Neil Alexander

Page 35 | Photograph Copyright © R'Evolution

Page 36 | Photograph Copyright © Phebe Huth

Page 39 | Photograph Copyright © Rush Jagoe

Page 45 | Photograph Copyright © Brennan's Chanteclair Room by Chris Granger

Page 46 | Photograph Copyright © Gautreau's

Page 51 | Photograph Copyright © Sylvain

Page 52 | Photograph Copyright © The Country Club

Page 57 | Photograph Copyright © Ace Hotel New Orleans

Page 59 | Photograph Copyright © J Collection Hotels

Page 62 | Photograph Copyright © Maison De La Luz by Stephen Kent Johnson

Page 65 | Photograph Copyright © Pontchartrain Hotel

Page 67 | Photograph Copyright © Soniat House

Page 69 | Photograph Copyright © The Chloe by Paul Costello

Page 70 | Photograph Copyright © The Ritz Carlton

Page 73 | Photograph Copyright © The Roosevelt New Orleans, A Waldorf Astoria Hotel

Page 75 | Photograph Copyright © Windsor Court by Marco Ricca

Page 78 | Photograph Copyright © Branbury Cross

Page 83 | Photograph Copyright © Pippen Lane

Page 88 | Photograph Copyright © Drink Beauty

Page 93 | Photograph Copyright © Pilot/Powell

Page 95 | Photograph Copyright © Sunday Shop

Page 104 | Photograph Copyright © The National WWII Museum

Page 107 | Photograph Copyright © New Orleans Museum of Modern Art

Page 113 | Photograph Copyright © Phebe Huth

Page 128 | Photograph Copyright © Phebe Huth

Page 133 | Photograph Copyright © Phebe Huth

Page 145 | Photograph Copyright © Melinda Stevens

Page 147 | Photograph Copyright © Waris Ahluwalia

Page 148 | Photograph Copyright © Chris Granger

Page 149 | Photograph Copyright © Alexa Pulitzer

Page 151 | Photograph Copyright © Roopal Patel

Page 152 | Photograph Copyright © Lauren Bush Lauren

Page 154-155 | Photograph Copyright © Sara Ruffin Costello by Paul Castello

Page 157 | Photograph Copyright © Gucci Westman

Page 158 | Photograph Copyright © Paul Castello

Page 159 | Photograph Copyright © Cece Villere Colhoun

Page 161 | Photograph Copyright © Claiborne Swanson Frank

Page 162 | Photograph Copyright © Lily Aldridge

Photographs of Jordan Rhodes | Copyrights © Julia D'Agostino

"

AN AMERICAN

HAS NOT SEEN THE

UNITED STATES UNTIL HE

HAS SEEN MARDI GRAS

IN NEW ORLEANS.

Mark Twain

ABOUT THE AUTHOR

Founder and Editor of Glimpse, Jordan Rhodes, is a wife and mother to three kids, living in Greenwich, CT. Exploring the world has always been an important part of her life, but she did not want to trade in the glamour of travel once she had kids in tow, so Jordan set out to find the most stylish hotels and restaurants that also welcomed her rambunctious toddlers. Along the way, Glimpse was born so that she could share her finds, interview a variety of globetrotters and tastemakers from many different industries, and provide travel tips for discerning families, all while promoting the importance of travel as education for young kids. In 2017, Jordan founded Give A Glimpse, which uses all profits from Glimpse to help fund educational travel opportunities for students in need.

Jordan loves to answer all travel-related questions, and can be found on Instagram @jordanjrhodes and @glimpseguides.

JORDAN'S NEW ORLEANS FAVORITES

My ideal day in New Orleans would begin by waking up at Soniat House and eating breakfast in the courtyard. I would then meander around the French Quarter, popping in and out of antique stores and voodoo shops, before making my way to the Garden District for more great finds. For lunch I'd head back to Galatoire's for several hours of food and drinks with friends, hoping that a jazz band will wander in off the streets and serenade the crowd, which is known to happen there. I would then head to NOMA or the WWII museum for a little culture, then drinks at The Chloe or Jack Rose, followed by dinner at Clancy's. Finally, I would head back to the French Quarter to soak in the street music and midnight revelers, and let the night lead the way.